THE WORLD
ACCORDING TO

YVESSAINTLAURENT

Edited by
Patrick Mauriès
Jean-Christophe Napias

Foreword by
Patrick Mauriès

Design and illustrations by
Isabelle Chemin

Illustration on the front cover and spine based on *Portrait of Yves Saint Laurent,* an original photograph by Jeanloup Sieff, 1969. © Estate of Jeanloup Sieff.

First published in the United Kingdom in 2023 by Thames & Hudson Ltd, 181A High Holborn, London WC1V 7QX

First published in the United States of America in 2023 by Thames & Hudson Inc., 500 Fifth Avenue, New York, New York 10110

The World According to Yves Saint Laurent
© 2023 Thames & Hudson Ltd, London

Edited compilation © 2023 Patrick Mauriès and Jean-Christophe Napias
Foreword © 2023 Patrick Mauriès

Illustrations and design by Isabelle Chemin

Translation by Bethany Wright

The authors would like to thank the Fondation Pierre Bergé – Yves Saint Laurent and the Musée Yves Saint Laurent Paris for access to their archives. Special thanks also to Madison Cox, President of the Fondation Pierre Bergé – Yves Saint Laurent, and the Musée Yves Saint Laurent Paris team – Elsa Janssen, Marie Delas, Alice Coulon-Saillard, Serena Bucalo-Mussely, Judith Lamas and Domitille Eblé – for their invaluable help during the preparation of this work.

British Library Cataloguing-in-Publication Data
A catalogue record for this book is available from the British Library

Library of Congress Control Number 2023938643

ISBN 978-0-500-02618-2

Printed and bound in China by C & C Offset Printing Co. Ltd

MIX
Paper | Supporting
responsible forestry
FSC® C008047

Be the first to know about our new releases,
exclusive content and author events by visiting
thamesandhudson.com
thamesandhudsonusa.com
thamesandhudson.com.au

CONTENTS

THE THREE FACES OF YVES SAINT LAURENT

As in Titian's famous work *The Allegory of Prudence*, the following pages paint a portrait of Yves Saint Laurent with three different faces: from the shy, determined prodigy of his early days at Dior, to the designer at the height of his powers in the 1970s, and finally the tormented soul, haunted by shadows, of his later years. As in Titian's painting, these three faces show how the attributes that make up what we call identity change, retreat or grow stronger as time goes by.

The first aspect of Saint Laurent's identity is that he was clearly born to be a couturier: he was one of those rare people whose fate is marked out from a young age by a handful of fleeting moments – a sketch of a tuxedo jacket, the rustle of a satin dress, a pair of red heels – which became etched into his memory and fuelled a single-minded, perhaps even blind, passion for the world of fashion. It is no coincidence that we find similar childhood memories recounted in the origin stories of many other designers, such as Christian Lacroix, Jean Paul Gaultier and Karl Lagerfeld, to name just a few of those who were close to Saint Laurent, in one way or another.

Where Saint Laurent differs from these designers, however, is that he belonged – to use one of his favourite quotes from Proust – to the 'family of neurotic people': he was marked out by his hypersensitive nature, his need for solitude, his sense of not having made the most of his youth and his impossible yearning to recapture it, which sometimes led him to indulge in harmful behaviours. It would be easy to view this extreme fragility as a weakness in his character, but in fact it shows the exact opposite: this paralysing vulnerability was the flip side of an innate self-confidence, a steely determination, a rare ability to assert himself. The teenage Saint Laurent held an 'unwavering faith and belief' in what he viewed as his destiny, and this allowed him to withstand the bullying and violence that marked his school days. He recalled, 'I was looking at my classmates and thinking: I will get my revenge on you, you will be nothing, I will be everything'.

Another paradox (which we also find with Coco Chanel and Cristóbal Balenciaga) lay in Saint Laurent's symbiotic relationship with fashion: the tension between, on the one hand, the need to embrace change and seek out novelty – which were driving forces of his career – and, on the other, the quest to refine his own style, a classic 'elegance' that provided a few fixed points in the maelstrom, a time-lessness that would come to define the couturier's creative spirit and his work. Saint Laurent's creative process was always a balancing act between his need to innovate and his desire to go deeper, to rework, to understand every detail of a design. We may appre-ciate the contrast between his process and that of

his eternal frenemy Karl Lagerfeld, who, throughout his career, chose not to revisit his designs from
earlier seasons or to seek to establish his own style,
preferring to adapt to different environments and to
play around with the signature styles of the couture
houses he was associated with, trying out multiple
identities in which he could lose himself.

The parallel, or rather the contrast, between
these two designers is invaluable; like a photo nega-
tive, it reveals the true nature of Yves Saint Laurent's
creative vision. The two couturiers were polar oppo-
sites in terms of their designs, their tastes, their ways
of life, the circles in which they moved, and how they
understood and practised their vocation. Everything
about them was in contrast: a centrifugal force and a
centripetal force, extreme fluctuations of mood and
a refusal to be defeated by them, the influence of the
past and an obsession with the present, nostalgia and
a longing to forget, the temptation to take risks and a
fear of losing control. And couture and spectacle,

as Saint Laurent would have added, not without a certain arrogance.

There is only one sentence, one statement of Saint Laurent's, that could have come from either designer, because Lagerfeld often professed the same inclination: 'I only feel comfortable at home, with my pencils and my papers'. But what for Lagerfeld was the prelude to socializing was for Saint Laurent simply another reason to retreat.

This sense of a fundamental contradiction, a need to engage with the present while at the same time remaining distant from it, formed a constant bass line to Saint Laurent's life. It draws together each of the three faces that we evoked at the start, imbuing the struggle with his demons that dominated his life with added poignancy, and inspiring creations that were a lavish, nostalgic celebration of femininity.

Patrick Mauriès

**YSL
ON
YSL
(1)**

I used to watch my mother whenever she went out. My mother was extraordinarily beautiful, with hair like Rita Hayworth. She had a red satin suit. Wonderful legs. Red shoes. My father wore a dinner jacket. These are memories that will stay with me forever.

My childhood refuses to die. It lives on in me, like a secret.

Youth is a sickness that often we do not recover from until very late in life. Indeed, some people never manage it. They die from it.

You know, I am an old child.

I had
a wonderful childhood.
I was a very sensitive,
very happy child.

I will be less so later in life.

Love
is
the best
cure
for
ageing.

I rebel often. I feel frustrated. I never had and will never have a chance to be young, to be carefree.

★

I am not the slightest bit vain about my age. I see life through the eyes of a child, and that is why I don't get old.

★

Youth is selfish. Growing older means starting to think of others.

★

I think there is only one true kind of happiness to be found on Earth. It lies in forgetting yourself and dedicating yourself to other people. When you try to make others happy, you end up getting some happiness reflected back at you.

★

Peace is a second youth to be enjoyed in old age. It is surely just as beautiful as actual youth. It is a luxury that lies within everyone's reach, the culmination of a life and a life's work. It is the opposite of a privilege.

YSL ON YSL (1)

During my teenage years, I felt a burning desire flare up inside me, to go to Paris and take over the city, to reach the highest echelons. I was looking at my classmates and thinking: I will get my revenge on you, you will be nothing, I will be everything.

I think I have remained true to the teenager who showed his first sketches to Christian Dior with unwavering faith and belief. I have never lost that faith and belief.

When I was twenty-one, I suddenly found myself locked in a kind of fortress built by fame. It would turn into a trap in which I was caught for the rest of my life.

Those around
me understood
straight away
that I was

different.

I only feel comfortable at home with my dog, my pencils and my papers.

You are never truly alone when you live among familiar shadows.

Nostalgia is a waking dream. I am a great dreamer.

Solitude. It's my driving force, but also a curse.

★

I love my friends but I don't see them often. But then, of course, it must be said that fame means loneliness.

★

I fight against loneliness because I love life. But perhaps life doesn't love me back!

*What is life? It's a thermometer with joy and
happiness at the top of the scale, and pain and
suffering at the bottom. And constantly oscillating
between these two extremes is a struggling heart.*

*You have to learn how not to ask too much
of life, how to appreciate everything it gives you.
Our failures generally come from asking too much
of life and not asking enough of ourselves.*

*The only possible source of meaning in human
existence is art. It is the only way we can hope
to achieve happiness.*

*Looking closely at how you live often leads to
vertigo, but experiencing this vertigo is how we
achieve a perfect balance.*

*My personal weapon is my ability to see the times
in which I live.*

I am a scandalous man, when all is said and done.

WHAT IS MY
GREATEST
FLAW?

Myself.

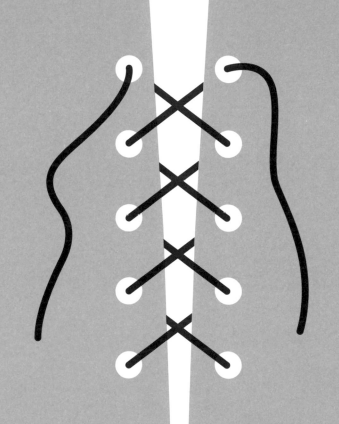

YSL
ON
FASHION

FASHION
changes,
BUT STYLE
is eternal.
FASHION
is fleeting,
BUT STYLE
is not.

Modern life is now so different, everything has changed so much that women no longer want to be transformed by wearing a different silhouette every season, or even every year. I think that fashion has reached a certain equilibrium.

For me, anyway, fashion is about a change of attitude. If you look at fashion throughout all the different eras, I think it's about changing attitudes among women. So I try, in my own small way, to change women's attitudes.

★

It is cruel: creating things that will never be seen again, things that by their very nature will disappear. Fashion means making things that go out of fashion...

★

With Chanel, I realized that good things don't go out of fashion.

I adore clothes, but I hate fashion.

★

*Fashion? We assign too much importance to it.
It's enough to drive you crazy.*

★

*Sometimes, I wonder what I'm doing, struggling
away. It's like putting on a crazy show, full of
horrors and not much fashion!*

★

Fashion has become something of a circus.

★

*Recently, fashion has become about putting on a
show. There are stages, musicians, sets, tricks, all
of which are designed to amaze people, to make an
impression rather than anything else. It's not about
the clothes any more, but about the spectacle. Often
the result is that the show can be perfect but the
dress is unwearable. It also means that names are
launched every year like hot air balloons, and then
next year the hot air balloons have disappeared.*

Fashion is an incurable disease

Fashion doesn't change.
We try to make people
believe that it does.
But some fashions
can transcend change,
can become works of art
that last forever.

But only some.

*Fashion is a kind of vitamin for style. It stimulates
you, it gets you going. But there's a risk of overdose.
It can destroy the balance of your personality –
that goes for a designer and also for the woman
who wears his clothes.*

*I don't see the point of changing the design of a
piece from one season to the next if it is working
perfectly well.*

*There is a kind of fashion that never changes and
then there is street fashion, which everyone can
be involved in. If tomorrow you have an idea, you
can become a stylist and achieve success, but you
will never be able to make a real piece of clothing.
That isn't possible for everyone. Anyone can create
fashion, but not very many people can create a real
piece of clothing.*

*Women who follow fashion too closely are running
a great risk – that of losing their true nature, their
style, their innate elegance.*

The time of the dictators is over. Fashion is no longer solely the domain of the rich. It no longer clings to class distinctions. Fashion cannot be cut off from life, it must draw inspiration from new, exciting ideas. Our goal is to appeal to women, to thrill them, not simply to clothe them. A fashion designer must capture the spirit of his time... A fashion designer must be a liberator. If we are interested in youth, it is because it has become a powerful force, a kind of cult dedicated to celebrating itself. And we, the young fashion designers, are the leaders of this cult.

★

In Africa, in Asia and in many Slavic countries, clothes do not change very much, and most of the time young women wear the same dresses as older women. This supports my theory that we can wear the same thing at any age.

When the revolution comes, it will be driven by young people. There is an abiding conflict between the generations... It's always like that in the fashion world... every twenty-five years the fashion community changes, the reference points change. A new generation is emerging.

FASHION
IS A
CELEBRATION.

Fashion is eternally youthful. It moves and transforms with the changing times. It is the mirror that reflects the soul of an era. It flourishes and dies with it, only to be reborn stronger, moving to the beat of the next new era.

There are two kinds of fashion: one that endures, that never goes out of style, such as trousers, trenchcoats, skirts, blouses and so on, a whole range of clothes that are becoming more and more standardized. In my opinion, that is what determines the style of a designer or an era. Then there is a more fun side that we call fashion, true fashion, made up of jokes, details that can change every season or every year. That is creativity.

We need playfulness, frivolity, humour, indulgence, contradictions. We need celebrations. Fashion should also be a celebration, it should give people a chance to play. To change. To escape. It should go some way towards softening this awful grey, hard world in which they are forced to live. It should clothe their dreams, their escapes, their extravagances.

YSL
ON
THE
CREATIVE
PROCESS

When I pick up a pencil, I don't know what I'm going to draw. What I mean is, nothing is ever planned in advance. It's a miracle, a moment of inspiration. A line. I start by drawing a woman's face, then suddenly the dress follows, the garment becomes clear in my mind, but it's not something I've thought about before. It's creation in its purest state, without planning, without following a vision.

★

Once I designed a whole collection in twenty days. Twenty days of pure creation, of pure madness, then one evening towards midnight, everything was finished. Sometimes it's much more painful, I have no inspiration, then something bursts out of me, and it's as if I am witnessing my own rebirth.

★

I have learned to be suspicious of inspiration, to avoid it like the plague. Little by little, I realized that fashion is not an art but a craft. Its starting point and its aim are rooted in something concrete: the female body.

Some days I can sit for a whole morning without picking up a pencil, then at other times an idea suddenly hits me and I draw forty designs.

Since my
first collection,
the Trapeze line,
I have been plagued
by constant fear.

Creating fashion with a sell-by date is no fun. All those dresses that are dead a year later and, at the same time, all those dresses you have to make. It's a graveyard and a foundry. I feel torn between life and death, between the past and the future.

★

Every time, you have to question all your assumptions. You can't afford to get it wrong in fashion. You don't have the luxury of being right in three or four years' time. You always have to be in touch with the outside world. We expect designers to feel everything that is going on around them and everything that is going to happen, and to translate it into their designs. I made the rope to hang myself with.

★

I have to say that when I'm designing, when I'm creating clothes, I feel pretty terrible. There's a constant fear, which is unfounded but overwhelming. My heightened sensitivity is what has given me this wonderful creative power, but at the same time it eats away at me.

I don't believe creative people are ever happy. The act of creating is a desperate attempt to communicate something you can't express through language.

★

All I can say is that I will never stop creating. It's my reason for living.

★

There is no creativity without pain. It's a happy thing, but the process of getting there is very painful. It's only happy once you've reached the end.

★

Wanting to be a creator means voluntarily diving into the depths of pain. It is true that there are some extraordinary moments. It is the happiness you feel when your lifeblood surges in your veins.

My
career
is the
backbone
of my
life.

The streets
and I,
it's a true
love story.

I think that nature gave me a gift, the gift of understanding what women desire at any given moment. I don't need to go out, to travel, or to seek distractions to kickstart my inspiration. I have always said that I have antennae and that all I need to do is open my bedroom window every morning and breathe in the Parisian air.

My greatest source of inspiration is watching what is happening in the world from an artistic, literary or political point of view, or simply watching women go by in the street. It's a very important source of inspiration for me, because it is life itself, and fashion is a reflection of everyday life.

It's important that there is also ugliness in the streets.

*I live in my head, I don't live in the world. Before,
I used to go out a lot, I would dance all night,
I had a fast car, like Sagan, but that's all over now.
I enjoyed that feverish existence, but it isn't part of
me any more. Now my soul is welded to my art. I live
solely through it and for it, and I find big occasions
inspire me less than pure beauty.*

*I am very, very solitary. I use my imagination to
travel to lands I have never visited. I hate travelling
in real life. For example, if I read a book about
South East Asia, with photos, or about Egypt, where
I've never been, my imagination takes me there.
That is how I go on my most beautiful journeys.*

*I am convinced that my imagination goes beyond
normal limits, that it takes me to places I don't need
to go. My most beautiful journeys don't actually
involve travelling anywhere.*

The most beautiful
journey, in the end,
is the one you take
around your room.

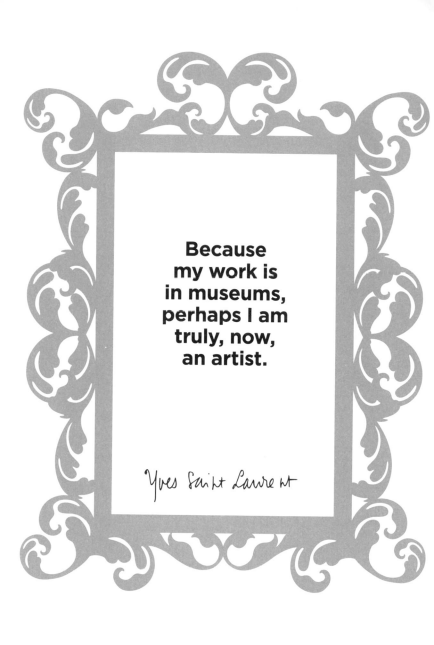

**Because
my work is
in museums,
perhaps I am
truly, now,
an artist.**

Yves Saint Laurent

Every art is defined by its medium, mine by clothing.

★

Art and creativity are the manifestations of divinity within humankind. The search for purity.

★

I have always placed the utmost importance on respecting this career which is not exactly an art but which needs an artist in order for it to exist.

★

Putting my imagination to work is very important to me. Looking at Girl with a Pearl Earring *by Vermeer, I imagined the dress she would wear. And I believe that it's one of the most beautiful dresses I've ever created.*

★

How can we create the beauty of the future if we neglect the beauty of the past and allow it to disappear?

YSL
ON
THE WORK
OF A
DESIGNER

There is no other career in which twice a year
you have to question everything you thought you
knew. Before each collection, I suffer from terrible
attacks of nerves, and with good reason. Since the
age of twenty, I have felt an overwhelming sense of
responsibility: if I get it wrong, hundreds of people
will lose their jobs.

Putting together a collection is a terrible moment.
It's a struggle every time, as if my inspiration has
dried up forever. And then, about two weeks before
the collection is due to launch, the floodgates open.
It's a truly euphoric moment.

For me, the creative process
has always been painful.
Not at the stage of first coming
up with the idea, or sketching it,
but when I have to breathe
life into a piece of fabric,
when I have only my scissors
and my pins and everything
seems flat, stupid, dead.
There is always a moment when
I want to tear everything up and run
off to live naked on a desert island,
when I want to forget the very
meaning of the words crepe,
velvet, satin and, worst of all,

collection.

*This is how
I want my
collections to be:
a spectacle.*

I also want to say that while you're working on a collection, it belongs only to you, it's sacred. But as soon as you entrust it to other people, you feel frustrated, almost violently so, as if it's been stolen from you. Then you feel depressed. Then that feeling begins to fade. Then comes the moment I like most of all: you feel joyful at having given something to the world, you see women wearing your clothes and the dresses come to life. And life goes back to normal.

People have no idea how difficult it is to create dresses. But now I have come into my own as a designer. It's something you feel suddenly: you have something that belongs only to you, that will never leave you. It's an amazing feeling.

After launching a collection, I feel drained. It has poured out of me and there is nothing left. It was made by my hands, but now it is something that people buy, that they wear, that they might throw away. A book, a painting, a song or a sculpture endure, but fashion... It's so frustrating to know that your work will not last!

I prefer to shock people rather than bore them by rehashing the same ideas.

★

I find it difficult to explain a collection because I always feel like I've done the same thing.

★

As I progress in my career, I am gaining more of the quality I have always dreamed of: this kind of suppleness and ease that I didn't have at all when I started out.

★

Sewing a sleeve, making a skirt, all these things that seem so simple but are so difficult, that's how you can tell someone is a true couturier.

★

Creating an illusion is an important part of a designer's work. This has always been my guiding principle.

★

It's outdated now to talk about a revolution in the fashion world. The true revolution is happening elsewhere. It is the revolution of the mind that will shape the fashion revolution.

For me,
the true
avant-garde,
is
classicism.

People see us as frivolous, although our work is meaningful and serious.

All my dresses are inspired by a gesture. A dress that doesn't reflect or make you think of a gesture is no good. Once you have found the right gesture, only then can you choose the colour, the shape, the fabric, not before. In this job, you never stop learning your craft.

Fashion must be amusing, modern and fun. But it is important for the designer to have knowledge, not only of couture, but also of history and art.

I believe that a designer who is not also a couturier, who has not learned the most refined mysteries of physically creating his designs, is like a sculptor who gives his drawings to another man, an artisan, to accomplish. For him, not completing the process of creation will always feel like an interrupted act of love, and his style will bear the shame of it, the impoverishment.

For me, the most beautiful achievement in fashion is creating a garment that has the simplicity and elegance of a black skirt and jumper. They are nothing and everything at the same time.

That is our job:

PRECISION, MODESTY, SERIOUSNESS, TIMELESSNESS.

I am not
a designer,
but a craftsman.

A maker of
happiness.

I thank heaven that I have become the designer that I am.

★

This is a career that causes a lot of harm, but also brings great joy.

★

It seems to me that the more I suffer, the more I need to make joyful things.

★

I have lived for my work and through my work.

YSL
ON
STYLE

STYLE

To define a look precisely – to describe what I see, what I'm interested in – I have to think about everything, from head to toe.

I think that the most important thing for a designer to have is their own recognizable style.

I have the same process as a painter, a sculptor, an architect or a musician. For a designer, this creative process means inventing a new look, breaking new ground, like Chanel, Balenciaga or Dior; put simply, it means finding and imposing your own style.

It's not enough to find your own style, you have to maintain it, refine it, breathe new life into it. Now, for example, I can design a blazer four times a year and make it different every time. It is through perfecting such staples that I honed my style, that I became what I am today. And that is why my work transcends fashion. That is also why women can wear dresses of mine that came out a long time ago without ever feeling they are outdated.

Elegance belongs to those who have gone in search of their own style. In life as in fashion.

For me, classic means eternal, timeless.

★

I am classic at heart and I like discipline.

★

The simpler a garment, the more perfect it is.

★

'Novelty' doesn't interest me very much. I am criticized for repeating myself, but that's a misunderstanding: in reality, I innovate every year but I retain the same line.

★

Nothing to me is more anti-style than revolutions in the way of dressing.

★

Only style allows you to go beyond fashion.

I AM NOT TRYING TO REVOLUTIONIZE FASHION, BUT TO REFINE, AGAIN AND AGAIN, THE IDEAL SILHOUETTE.

I feel like I am always
doing the same thing
doing the same thing
doing the same thing
doing the same thing
doing the same thing
doing the same thing

but in fact, that's
not the case at all.

What is most important in my work? It's style. I don't change, I delve deeper. Cuts change. Fashions change, but style endures.

My true style draws on men's fashion. That is why my style is androgynous. I realized that men felt much more confident in their clothes, and women were not as confident. So I tried give them this confidence, to give them a strong silhouette.

Just as an artist finds his own style, a woman must find hers. And once she has found it, whatever the current trends are, she is sure to possess a certain seductive power.

Style is a silhouette. A line. Fashion is ephemeral but style always remains.

My task is to arrive at the fullest sense of purity.

YvesSaintLaurent

haute couture

YSL
ON
HAUTE
COUTURE

I LIKE
SOPHISTICATION.

I HATE

For me, haute couture is not a laboratory experiment, as people often say, but an exercise in style in which you achieve a level of perfection that is unattainable in ready-to-wear fashion.

Haute couture is a mistress that I cannot do without, and I feel a responsibility towards the people who made me and my fashion house a success.

It is necessary because it is a genuine craft and it is important to preserve craftsmanship in an era of standardization, an era that is leaning more and more towards industrialization. Also because it is about luxury and originality, as opposed to uniformity. At the heart of each of us there is a need to stand out.

Haute couture is the pinnacle of this industry. If you love fashion, it is in haute couture that you can attain the highest form of perfection. So it's very important to me, and I don't imagine I will ever turn my back on it.

Haute couture is luxury and finesse; ready-to-wear fashion is life. It has brought an injection of youth into my collections, while haute couture adds a touch of refinement.

For as long as I can, I will make both practical clothes for the ready-to-wear market and dreamlike creations for haute couture.

Haute couture is no longer influential. What is influential now is fashion that can be bought straight away, by anyone.

I think that ready-to-wear fashion is the future, because the future is full of hope, full of novelty.

I decided to express
my identity as a designer
through my ready-to-wear
collections rather than
my haute couture... I think
ready-to-wear lines are the
embodiment of fashion
today. That is where its
essence truly lies, not in
haute couture.

In 1966, I was the first couturier in the world to open a ready-to-wear boutique. By designing clothes without reference to haute couture, I know that I moved the fashions of my time forward and gave women access to a world that had previously been shut off from them.

★

What I would really like is to be a chain like Prisunic, and to make much less expensive dresses, so that anyone can wear them, anyone can afford to buy them.

★

For a long time now, I have been convinced that the purpose of fashion is not only to make women look beautiful, but also to reassure them, to give them confidence, to allow them to be comfortable in their own skin. I have always objected to the flights of fancy from certain designers who use fashion to stoke their own egos. In contrast, I have always wanted to be of service to women. To serve them. To serve their bodies, their gestures, their attitudes, their lives. I wanted to walk alongside them through this great wave of liberation that we've experienced over the last century.

**THAT IS WHY
I OPENED
A BOUTIQUE,
SO THAT I WOULD
NO LONGER BE JUST
A GREAT COUTURE DESIGNER.**

rive gauche

I am convinced that we are on the brink of a seismic change to our way of life, as revolutionary as the changes called for in the first Art Deco exhibition.

Down with the Ritz,

down with the moon,

long live the streets!

People have to change their own lives, minds and manner of living before they can change their clothes.

I think that, although for a short time people wanted to blend in with the crowd, to lose themselves in the anonymity of a uniform, now they want to stand out, to dress themselves for a role like a celebrity. And they want to emphasize their 'gender'. Boys want to grow a beard and girls want to express their intrinsic femininity.

I'm not sure exactly what a new type of fashion might look like, and what I could and could not accomplish within it, because that would mean abandoning everything I've made so far and starting all over again. I have a premonition of a kind of enormous door opening onto the world of ready-to-wear clothing, which will be the future of fashion, and which could transform it into something surprising, radically different and gigantic.

Haute couture is a discipline, but it's also a whisper that is passed down and repeated, we whisper our secrets to each other: the elegant finishing touches, our understanding of the cut. That is when haute couture becomes an art form; this sophistication is what has earned France its prestige and reputation for flair. Whatever he does elsewhere, a couturier must be anointed in Paris. Otherwise he will fade away.

★

When haute couture dies out, it will be the end of the last great crafts.

★

I am the last great couturier, haute couture will end with me.

Haute couture is a hoard of secrets that we whisper amongst ourselves. There are only a select few who have the privilege of passing them on.

YSL
ON
ELEGANCE

I belong to a generation and a world that are devoted to elegance, I grew up in an environment that placed great importance on traditions. At the same time, however, I wanted to change all that, because I was torn between the charm of the past and the future that propelled me forward. I feel like I am split in two and I think I will always feel that way. Because I know one world and I feel the presence of another.

Nowadays, a well-dressed woman is one who can match her clothes to her personality. The most elegant woman I know? Coco Chanel.

Elegance means completely forgetting what you are wearing. There are a thousand definitions, a thousand possible interpretations. Above all, it is a person's character that counts. The elegance of their actions, of their heart, have nothing to do with wearing expensive clothes. How terrible would it be if it was only about that.

Elegance is a way of moving. It is also about being able to adapt to every circumstance in life. Without an elegant heart, there is no elegance.

What is elegance?

I have a whole host of definitions. If I had to sum it up, perhaps I would say that above all

it is a way of life,

a way of moving through life, physically and morally.

The word
'*seduction*'
has, if you like,
replaced the word
'*elegance*'.
Everything has changed.
It's a certain way of
life,
rather than a certain way of
dressing.

Elegance has changed, and seduction has taken its place.

I don't like the word 'elegant'. I find it just as outdated as the term 'haute couture'.

I am not the one who has changed. The world has changed. It will never stop changing, so we are condemned endlessly to recalibrating our ways of seeing, of feeling, of judging. Certainty, peace, a clear conscience, that's all over. And elegance is also gone. Why should a group of old men with grey beards feel they have the right to decree, in the name of elegance, that this thing is good and that thing is bad?

Seduction: loving yourself a little makes you much more attractive. The most beautiful make-up a woman can wear is passion.

Trickery is a part of seduction. A woman is more affecting, and therefore more seductive, when she makes use of a little artifice.

A dress fulfils its purpose when it becomes in some way invisible... when you no longer see anything but the woman wearing it.

I think that women's two greatest weapons in the game of seduction are charm and mystery.

What counts
is seduction,

IMPACT.

What we feel,
what we sense.
It's purely subjective.
Personally, I am more
sensitive to gestures
than to looks,
the silhouette
or anything else.

WHEN YOU FEEL GOOD IN A PIECE
OF CLOTHING, ANYTHING CAN HAPPEN.
A GOOD PIECE OF CLOTHING IS A

PASSPORT

TO HAPPINESS.

A woman who has not yet found her style, who doesn't feel comfortable in her clothes, who doesn't live in harmony with them, is a sick woman. She is not happy, not sure of herself, and does not possess any of the characteristics that are necessary for happiness. We speak of the silence of health, the wonderful silence of health. We could also speak of the silence of clothes, the wonderful silence of clothes, I mean the moment when body and clothes become one, when you completely forget what you are wearing, when your clothes don't speak to you, I mean they don't cling to you, when you feel as comfortable clothed as you do when you are naked. This perfect harmony between body and clothes is rarely achieved without a perfect harmony between mind and body, between clothes and mind. Doesn't elegance mean completely forgetting what you are wearing?

It is not an easy thing to find your style. But once you have found it, there is no greater happiness. It means guaranteed confidence for life.

YSL
ON
WOMEN

I have always looked to women when developing my style. What gives it its vitality and strength is the fact that I base it on women's bodies, their movements, how their bodies are put together.

I think I have done everything I could for female emancipation.

I came up with a few key staples that I have returned to again and again in my collections over the past twenty years: blazers, pea coats, striped jerseys, mackintoshes, trouser suits, blouses, safari jackets and tuxedos, which allow women to feel at all times just as comfortable as men.

My dream is to give women the essentials that make up a classic wardrobe, not to pander to passing trends, but to give them more confidence in themselves. I hope that my clothes make them happier.

I invented the
modern woman.
I invented her past,
and I gave her
her future.

I never design abstractions, just clothes that live on a woman. What is important is the body – I love the body of a woman.

★

I cannot stand the idea of treating women as if they are not women, as if the designer were more important than the dresses. That shows an utter lack of respect.

★

I love all fabrics that display the female form. I love fabrics that move with the body. I love being able to see through the fabric, being able to make out the shape of a woman's body. Because the most important thing in couture, in fashion, is the body that you are dressing, the woman you are dressing, not the ideas that you may have.

★

The most beautiful thing a woman can wear is the arms of the man she loves. But for those women who are not lucky enough to find such happiness, that is why I am here.

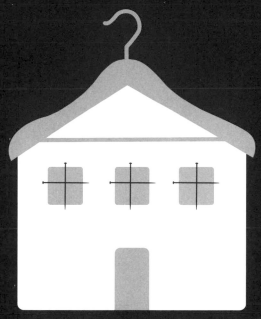

A dress is not a piece of 'architecture', it is a house: it is not made to be looked at, but to be lived in, and the woman who lives in it must feel beautiful and happy. Everything else is simply a flight of fancy.

I don't search at all for

AN

ideal woman,
but

SEVERAL

ideal women.

It is important to think of different types of women when creating, in order to achieve a universality of design.

★

I want to hold up a mirror to our time, to show women what they look like. The time when women changed their entire wardrobe every six months is over. Today, women's clothes never go out of fashion, and when I see women combining old designs of mine with clothes that I have just released, I like that a lot. Women are becoming more and more liberated, and we shouldn't seek to confine them.

★

For me, the ideal woman is an international woman, I mean all women combined into one... It's difficult to combine all women into one.

Clothing a woman's naked body without restricting her natural freedom of movement, that is my job. It's a tender dialogue between this naked woman and all the magical charms of these swathes of fabric.

For a woman to be easy to dress she must have a neck, shoulders and legs. I'll take care of the rest. A piece of clothing hangs from, hinges on, the shoulders. They need to be square and angular.

I don't think that the modern woman is a curvy woman. The woman of today has bones – she is all skin and bone. In the nineteenth century, the ideal woman was made up of curves. Curves are over now. That was Renoir's territory.

It is always the female body that emerges victorious. And I hide behind her, erase all traces of myself so as not to betray the truth of my work, the profound truth of how humble my ideas are when faced with the reality of the female body.

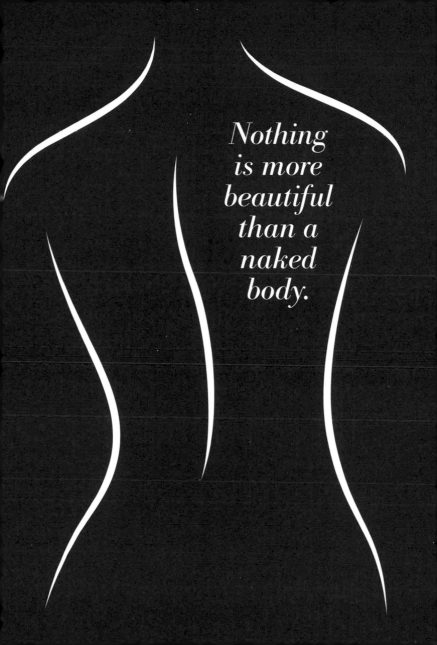

Nothing is more beautiful than a naked body.

Why
are you always asking
me about women?

Because I'm a
couturier?

I adore women. Maybe it is just because of my mother, or my education. I love to seduce women, and I prefer the company of women to that of men.

★

It is very important for a couturier to surround himself with beautiful women!

★

I believe that I created the modern woman's wardrobe, that I played a part in shaping the era in which I live. I did it through clothes, which is certainly less important than music, architecture, painting or many other art forms, but, be that as it may, I did it.

★

There are women who have completely transformed my view of fashion.

★

I would like to thank the women who have worn my clothes, the famous women and the unknown ones, who have been so faithful to me and have brought me such joy.

★

My life is a love story with women.

YSL
ON
MODELS

I have always been interested in women's dresses. When I was a young child, I played with figurines that were called 'my dolls' and I enjoyed dressing them up. Then I made them act out shows in an old puppet theatre set that must have been lying around in the attic. Even today, I still associate fashion with theatre. There is an element of performance in couture because models walking the runway have to be choreographed as in a ballet.

Each of my models represents a type of ideal woman to me.

What inspires
me is
BEAUTY.
Not the beauty
of the
dresses.
But the
BEAUTY
of the models
in the
dresses.

For me, a piece of clothing has to come alive,

and I need
a female body
to show how it will fit
into daily life.

*I need to have a female body in front of me. I need to
see how a woman holds herself, to see her elegance.
I base everything on her movements, on how her
body is put together, when I create a dress. That's
what gives it vitality and strength. I work with two
or three models to create the collection, then the
dresses are placed on other models who come in
at a later stage.*

★

*My models play a unique role because they represent
different kinds of women, and I draw a lot of
inspiration from their bodies, their movements, their
gestures. Sometimes, I get an idea for a dress simply
from the way a woman, a model, touches the fabric.
It's rather like in the bullring, you know, the model
is the bull and the designer is the matador.*

★

*There is a deep affinity between me and my models,
and between each model and the clothes that she
wears, because there are certain garments that a
model's body spontaneously rejects, I mean that
don't suit her. Sometimes I put them on other models
who they suit better, and sometimes they are bad
pieces that don't suit anyone.*

*I adore my models. There is a tenderness to the way
we work together. Everything they wear, everything
they are comes from me. At first, when I am starting
work on a collection, they are nervous, but I reassure
them and they relax, and then we are happy.
With men, I wouldn't be able to foster this kind
of miraculous bond.*

★

*People have no idea of the unspoken personal bond
that develops between a designer and a model.
Models can sense when my imagination is clicking
into gear, they are proud of the fact that their body,
their gestures, their appearance spark this creative
instinct in me.*

The choice of model
is very important to me.
I wrap the fabric around their body
and suddenly an idea hits me.
I talk to them very little
but I truly love them;
they are all in love with me.

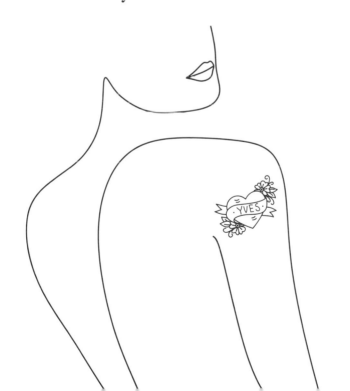

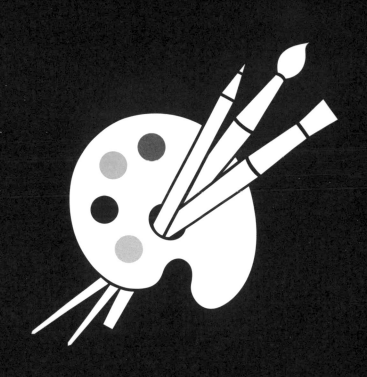

YSL
ON
COLOUR

I designed my first dress for my mother. It was a black organza cocktail dress. I already loved black.

Black was the essence of my first collections. Long black lines that symbolized pencil strokes on a white page: the silhouette in its purest form.

For me, black is a refuge because it expresses what I want. Everything becomes much simpler, more linear, more dramatic.

I like black because it is definite, it creates an outline, a clear style: a woman in a black dress is like a pencil stroke.

★

A woman is never more beautiful than when she is wearing a black skirt and jumper and is on the arm of the man she loves.

I TURN BLACK

I return again and again to the idea of a black veil made from chiffon or tulle. It creates an air of mystery... The mystery of a woman that we want to uncover by lifting her veil.

I love black, black is my favourite colour. I think that a white page is very boring and without black there are no pencil strokes, so there is no line. That is why I often dress women in black, because I like it when women look like drawings, like sketches.

Black is synonymous with line. And the line is the most important thing. That is what defines the look.

It's a wonderful colour. It allows you to create a purity of line, which you cannot achieve with any other colour.

INTO A COLOUR.

Before, I expressed myself mainly
in black, I was afraid of colour.
I didn't know how to use it – or
at least, I thought I didn't know
how to use it. It wasn't until, when
I was still very young, early on in
my career, I went to Morocco, and
Marrakesh in particular, that I
started to use colour in my work.
It was the colours of Morocco that
opened up that world for me.

*It took a long time for me to get comfortable
with colour.*

★

*I suddenly realized that dresses should no longer
be made up of lines but of colours. I realized that
we should no longer think of a piece of clothing as
a sculpture and that, instead, we should see it as a
child's mobile. I realized that up until then fashion
had been paralyzed and from now on we had to get
it moving.*

★

*Oran... a shimmering city, a patchwork of
a thousand colours under the balmy North
African sun.*

★

*On every street corner in Marrakesh, you come
across groups of men and women wearing intense,
striking colours, a jumble of pink, blue, green and
purple kaftans. And you would think these groups
had been drawn or painted, they are reminiscent
of sketches by Delacroix, but it's amazing to think
that in fact they are simply thrown together by the
random improvisations of life.*

After black, my favourite colour is pink.

★

Pink. It's a beautiful colour because it evokes childhood.

★

This reflection of the sky and sun in the mirror, I would like to make that into an evening dress.

★

I love gold, a magical colour for a woman's reflection, the colour of the sun.

★

I love red, aggressive and wild, and beige, the colour of the desert.

★

Gold, because it is pure and it flows like liquid, moulding to the body until the body becomes nothing more than a line.

Red,
forms the basis of make-up,
the lips and nails.

Red,
is a noble colour, the colour
of a precious stone – ruby –
and it's a dangerous colour –
sometimes you have to play
with fire.

Red,
is a religious colour,
it stands for blood,
and it's regal,
it represents Phaedra
and a whole host of
mythical heroines.

Red,
symbolizes fire and fight,
red
is like a battle between
life and death.

Matisse convinced me of the merits of colour, because when I was starting out, I only trusted black.

For my work, as for a painter, light is crucial.

Velázquez's dresses, for example, are like oceans.
I admire Manet's rich, complex whites.

Picasso's work is pure genius. It is brimming with
life and truth. Picasso is not about purity. His work
is baroque. It has many streams, many arcs, many
strings to his bow.

When it comes to colours, I was greatly inspired
by Braque and Matisse. When I'm designing a
collection, the fabrics all arrive, the silks are laid
out in front of me, and suddenly I see a colour, I find
it wonderful, I pick it out and I make a dress.

Mondrian's work is about purity, and it is the height
of purity in painting. His work has the same purity
found in the Bauhaus. The greatest masterpiece of
the twentieth century is a Mondrian.

YSL
ON
ACCESSORIES

*In my mind, accessories make a piece of clothing
into a coherent outfit, and at the same time they
ensure a look is unique.*

★

*Elegance is not simply about clothes, or about
wealth, obviously. It's about how a woman moves,
how she looks, it's an effortlessness that suddenly
lends her a certain confidence. For example,
a woman wearing a jet-and-diamanté belt with a
black skirt and jumper, a black chiffon scarf around
her neck, lots of bracelets, black stockings and
black shoes, for me that is the height of elegance.
Dressed like that, a woman is comfortable in her
clothes, and her character comes from her unusual
accessories and jewellery. A woman who has no
personality is lost, she is afraid of fashion, she
cannot find her own style.*

You can never overstate the
importance of accessories.
They transform a dress.
I like pairing an
unassuming dress
with a crazy accessory.

I like gold buttons.

I think they are a kind

of daytime jewellery

for women.

Accessories transform a woman, a dress. I like bracelets – for example, African bracelets or Cretan gold cuff bracelets – strings of gold necklaces, coral, jade, black patent-leather belts, black stockings, chiffon scarves, ribbons and high heels – a classic black snakeskin shoe can be the foundation of an entire outfit. And I like pearls.

No precious stones, no colours, no sequins. Just gold, or preferably gilt, because I only like costume jewellery. For me, a belt is a piece of jewellery, not something to cinch in the waist.

When accessorizing, I think of Ingres and Delacroix. I imagine the dress that Vermeer's Girl with a Pearl Earring *would have been wearing, because in the museum in Amsterdam you see her only from the shoulders up.*

*What ages a woman is not her wrinkles or her
white hair, but the way she moves. That is where
accessories play an important role.*

*My accessories are movements. A scarf that you can
play with, a bag with a strap that leaves your hands
free – there is nothing uglier than a bag held in one
hand. A supple belt – a chain belt, always – that
makes a woman's hips sway prettily, and pockets.
Pockets are very important. Take two women both
wearing a long jersey tube dress. The woman who
has pockets will immediately feel superior to the
one without.*

*I like the movements a woman makes when playing
with her gloves.*

*Every woman imbues her clothes with a different
personality depending on whether she accessorizes
them in one way or another.*

GLOVES,
like jewellery,
are a true
source of
PASSION.

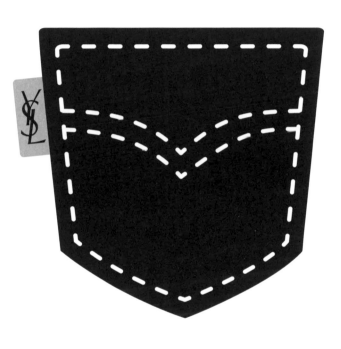

FROM JEANS
TO
TUXEDO
JACKETS

I am not at all afraid of jeans. I think they're a wonderful piece of clothing. They are kind of the clothes of our time.

★

The beatniks showed us the elegance of a pair of blue jeans.

★

The clothes for our times, for example, are a pair of jeans. They were not born of a passing trend, they were not created by a designer for a season, they are something lasting. Just like trousers, jumpers. I have made denim clothes, but I will never achieve the perfection of the original.

★

After jeans, there is nowhere else to go. Nowhere. They are the perfect marriage of a piece of clothing and an era. This harmony is very important.

★

Before, I was a slave to tradition. Now, by giving women the chance to be like teenagers in a pair of blue jeans, I give them the illusion of youth. I have managed to set them free by giving them a new outlook. A new way of combining things.

I'd love to invent something
that comes
after jeans.

There must
surely be
something.

Not every
woman
can wear
trousers,
but nor
can every
woman
wear every
dress.

A woman in trousers is seductive only if she wears them with all her femininity. Not like George Sand. Trousers are a kind of flirtation, an added charm, not a symbol of equality, of emancipation. Freedom and equality can't be gained by wearing a pair of trousers, they're a state of mind.

When I introduced trousers, it caused a stir in America.

I think that if one day you had to choose a single picture to encapsulate women in the 1970s, it would have to be a woman in trousers.

I once saw a photograph of Marlene Dietrich in a man's suit and it left a lasting impression on me. A woman who dresses like a man – whether she is wearing a tuxedo, a blazer or a navy uniform – must be terribly feminine to be able to wear clothes that are not designed for her.

A woman in a trouser suit is very far from being masculine. The uncompromising, severe cut allows her femininity, her seductiveness, her ambiguity, to shine through even more strongly. She evokes the body of a teenager, I mean she taps into this powerful movement that is overturning tradition and inevitably leading to the uniformity and equality of the sexes. This androgynous woman, whose clothes make her the equal of a man, shakes up the traditional, classic, outdated image of femininity, and uses all the secret weapons that belong only to her (especially make-up and hair styling) to overcome what appears to be a disadvantage, but what is in fact simply the mysterious, seductive image of a modern woman.

Since 1966, when I launched the first tuxedo jacket in my collection, the idea of a woman wearing a man's suit has only grown stronger, it has intensified and established itself as the emblem of the modern woman.

If I had to choose

one item

from among all those that I have designed,
without doubt it would be the

tuxedo jacket

...It's almost the
Yves Saint Laurent

trademark

For a woman,
A TUXEDO
is an essential piece of
clothing that will always
make her feel fashionable,
because it is about style
and not about trends.
Trends change.
Style is eternal.

Street fashions change more quickly than the world of high fashion. I realized this five years ago when I released my first tuxedo jacket. In the world of couture, it was a failure. But in the ready-to-wear world, it was incredibly successful.

The tuxedo, which I popularized in 1968 and reworked in 1981, and which has always remained important to me, is a piece of clothing that will last forever.

I like luxury only when it is pared down. A girl in a black tuxedo. A long black jersey dress in the middle of a crowd of embroidery and sequins. People are always too overdressed.

Christian D.
Gabrielle C.
Cristóbal B.
Hubert de G.
Elsa S.

YSL
ON
DIOR,
CHANEL
AND
OTHER
DESIGNERS

For me, working for Christian Dior was like a miracle had taken place. I had endless admiration for him... He taught me the roots of my art. I owe him a major part of my life, and no matter what happened to me later, I never forgot the years I spent at his side.

★

Dior is like a beautiful painting that you hang on the wall... Dior means elaborate decoration, splendour, the baroque.

★

He taught me everything I needed to know. Later, other influences came along and, because he had given me this foundation, they added to it... and found wonderful fertile ground, already sown with the seeds that would allow me to find my voice, to grow in confidence, to spread my wings, to finally breathe life into a universe of my own creation.

I could never bring myself
to call him

Christian,

He was always

*Monsieur
Dior*.

I am very flattered that

Mademoiselle Chanel

deigned to show an interest in what I was doing and named me her heir, but I don't agree at all with her claim that I copied her. First of all, if I copied her, I would not be successful in the slightest.

Instead of designing outfits that trapped women in short-lived, clichéd trends, Chanel always sought to create fashion that would endure, that would be timeless. When I realized this, it helped me to shake off certain bad habits as a designer, and I started to rely less on sketches and to look more at the body and fabric.

★

The big difference between myself and Mademoiselle Chanel is that I try to design dresses that women can imbue with their own style, so that they can show their own personality. Whereas a woman who wears Chanel looks like Mademoiselle Chanel. There is another big difference between the two of us, and it is that I love the time in which I live, I love night clubs although I don't go often, I love the pop music that she calls 'yé-yé', I love clothes shops, I love everything that defines our era, and it all has a huge influence on what I do.

There are two kinds of designer that I cannot stand:
firstly, the kind who plays at being an alchemist,
hiding away in his laboratory in a white coat and
invoking Le Corbusier before designing the slightest
trinket. Those designers are far too unsophisticated.
Secondly, the kind of designer who wants to create
an air of mystery, who you never see and who
never sees anything, who is cut off from his time.
Both are wrong.

★

I think there are three kinds of designers. There are
the great designers, the true designers, the ones who
know how to delight a woman by making a very
simple dress, or a very simple suit. Then there are the
ones I call 'dressmakers', the workhorses making an
honest living. They're very boring, very bourgeois.
And then there are the self-proclaimed mavericks,
the kind of people who are always showing off, who
need to listen to music all the time, who wear Mickey
Mouse ears, who deck women out in scrap metal and
leather... the kind of thing that I don't understand,
that doesn't make any sense to me at all.

I
MAKE
CLOTHES,

not costumes.

*There are very
few great designers,
very few*

BRILLIANT
DESIGNERS

*Very, very few.
To be precise, I would say
that there have been two,
only two:*

GIVENCHY
AND
MYSELF.

*The rest, the others,
they're a mob, they're terrible.
That is precisely what 'fashion' is.
A void.*

Karl Lagerfeld did very well with Chanel. As for the others, I don't like them.

I had become mired in traditional ideas of elegance, and Courrèges pulled me out of that. His collection sparked something in me. I thought: 'I can do better'.

My aim was not to measure myself against the master couturiers, but to draw near to them and learn from their genius.

I'll freely admit that I don't greatly admire my fellow haute couture designers. All the ones I admired are dead.

I would like to pay tribute to those who guided my steps and served as an example to me. Firstly, Christian Dior, who was my mentor and the first person to reveal to me the secrets and mysteries of haute couture. Balenciaga, Schiaparelli. Chanel, of course, who taught me so much and who, as we know, set women free. Which paved the way for me, years later, to empower them and, in some way, to set fashion free.

Chanel understood women! She understood the time in which she lived and she created the woman of her time, and that is partly why she said that I was her only true heir. When she died, I became much more successful because my style began to blossom.

Balenciaga was all about style, about boldness, his work was very provocative and sensual. Dior was an extraordinary man and he had a certain boldness, but it was not that same confrontational boldness, like a slap in the face.

What I miss most is not having any giants left to slay. Faced with Givenchy, Balenciaga, Chanel, I had to rise to new heights.

I am the only one left,
after forty-two years.
The only one still here,
still working away.
The last couturier.
The last fashion house.

YSL
ON
PROUST

Marcel Proust...
his work saturates
every part of
my life.

*Creating something is painful, all year long I suffer
while I work. I shut myself away like a hermit,
I don't go out, it's a hard life and that's why I
understand Proust so well, I admire so much what
he wrote about the pain of creating. I remember
a sentence from* In the Shadow of Young Girls in
Flower: *'In the depths of what pain had he found
this unlimited power to create?' And I could quote
others, wonderful quotes about this same suffering,
quotes that I have copied out and framed and put
above my desk on the avenue Marceau.*

*He was completely consumed by his work,
he suffered greatly and sacrificed his life so that
his work would be the most perfect it could be,
the most surprising.*

*I think that I could have been friends with him, but
he was a very difficult person… Perhaps he wouldn't
have wanted me as a friend.*

155

YVES SAINT LAURENT'S RESPONSES
TO THE PROUST QUESTIONNAIRE (1968):

What is your main personality trait?
Willpower.

Your greatest flaw?
Shyness.

Your favourite quality in a man?
Indulgence.

And in a woman?
The same.

Your favourite historical figure?
Mademoiselle Chanel.

Your heroes in real life?
The people I admire.

What would you have liked to be?
A beatnik.

What is your idea of earthly happiness?
Sleeping with the people I like.

And the depths of misery?
Loneliness.

Where would you like to live?
Somewhere sunny, by the sea.

What gift would you like to have?
Physical strength.

What flaw do you find it easiest to forgive?
Betrayal.

Who is your favourite artist?
Picasso.

Your favourite musician?
Bach… and the musicians of the nineteenth century, opera composers.

And what authors do you like, other than Proust?
I love Proust so much that it's difficult for me to allow space for other writers. But I also love Céline and Aragon.

What is your favourite colour?
Black.

What do you hate more than anything else?
The snobbery of the rich.

And do you have a motto?
I would say Noailles's motto: 'More honour in the singular than honours in the plural.'

Of all writers, Proust is the one who wrote about women with the greatest sensitivity and truth. What impresses me most in Proust's work is not how skilfully he described dresses, but how he drew characters.

I love women and their beauty. I would like to make them even more beautiful, let them shine even brighter. Just like Marcel Proust, whom I love: nobody has ever described women as wonderfully as he did.

I like all of

PROUST'S WORK,

*but what I find particularly
interesting are the 'evenings at
Madame Verdurin's', because I
like the way Proust highlights
the smallest details to describe
the scene, how he re-creates an entire
lost atmosphere. The way a person
rests their elbow on the table,
the way they hold their cup...
the atmosphere rather than the
characters' psychology.*

I read Proust again and again...
I don't ever grow tired of it.
I pick up Proust and, in a way,
I get a sort of answer to my worries
and my questions.

At eighteen years old, I started reading In Search
of Lost Time. *I often pick up the book again, but
I never finish it. I need to have this extraordinary
work still ahead of me. I have a kind of superstitious
belief that if I finish reading it, something
will happen, nothing good. Perhaps I will die,
who knows?*

*I never want to finish [*In Search of Lost Time*].
I go back and start reading it again from halfway
through. I think that when I finally finish it,
something inside me will break. I'm still waiting.
And yet I am very tempted.*

YSL
ON
YSL
(2)

What I am always chasing, even unconsciously, is my work, and I know that to create it, I need to cut myself off, to concentrate in silence. I also know that you don't become a legend without producing a body of work, and as I said when I was still very young, I want to become a legend.

When I was at Dior, people called me 'the heir'. The press christened me 'the Little Prince'. My father called me 'my king'. Now, I am seen as a mythical figure. These crowns sometimes weigh heavily on my head.

You cannot steal success. At the most, you can deserve it or you can let down your admirers.

I love myself a little so that I can be liked greatly by others. It's very important to be liked. Everyone wants that.

I have a lot of love within me and I get a lot of love in return.

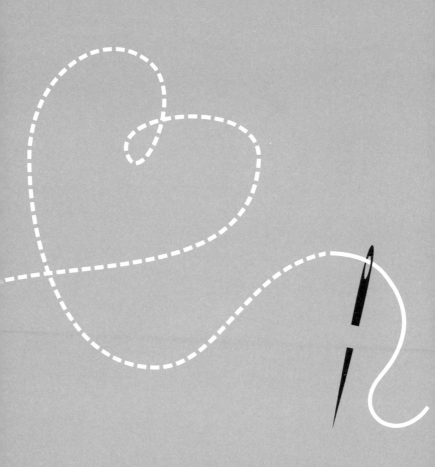

My heart is the
driving force behind
my entire life.

A hundred years
from now, I would
like people to study
my dresses,
my sketches.

*I am not aware of being a legend and I am still
surprised when people recognize me in the street.*

*Luckily there is a destructive kind of suffering
I've never known, the one that comes from lack
of recognition.*

*It's incredible, but young people like me very much.
I am very popular with young people, even very
young people, and I think it is because I have
always held on to the part of me that is childlike
and youthful, and that means I am like them.*

*I don't draw very well, I am not very expressive.
I would have liked to be a painter... but there are
so many things I would have liked to be!*

★

*I would have liked to be a writer. There was a time
when I wrote a lot. And then I stopped because it
wasn't possible to do both things at the same time,
to write as well as pursuing this terrifying career
that paralyzes me for most of the year. My mind is
full of dresses.*

★

*I was trying to decide between theatre and fashion.
It was meeting Christian Dior that pushed me
towards fashion.*

★

*I was spoiled by destiny. I have done exactly,
precisely what I wanted to.*

If I hadn't
been a designer,
I would definitely
have gone into
the theatre.

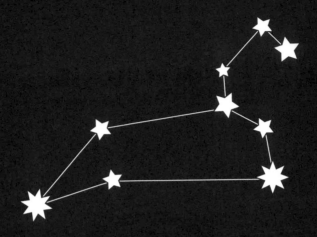

The future?

I never think about it.
I know that I have a future.
It is waiting for me somewhere,
I will go to meet it.
That's all.

Regrets? No, I don't have any regrets... Except for regretting the fact that time passes, that things disappear and don't come back.

★

I spent forty years trying to find myself, and sometimes I feel I am still searching.

★

I have suffered many bouts of depression over the years, but I have always managed to overcome them. There is a strength in me, a fierce determination, which pushes me towards hope and light. I am a fighter and a winner.

★

When I look back, I remember my youth, my nights out, my wild parties. And I smile.

★

I am not afraid of death. I know that death can strike at any moment, but, although it's strange and probably selfish, I don't feel that it would destroy my life.

*I have experienced many torments, many hells.
I have known fear and terrible loneliness. The false
friends of sedatives and narcotics. The prison cells
of depression and asylums. Then one day I emerged
from all that, dazed but sober.*

★

*Marcel Proust taught me that 'the magnificent
and pitiable family of neurotic people is the salt
of the earth'. Without realizing it, I was part of
this family. It is my family. I did not choose this
destructive lineage, but it is what has enabled
me to reach the heights of creativity, to rub
shoulders with the thieves of fire, as Rimbaud
calls them, to find myself. It is how I have realized
that the most important encounter in our lives is
the encounter we have with ourselves. The most
beautiful paradises are the ones we have lost.*

I won't forget you.

Yves Saint Laurent

Farewell speech, 7 January 2002

SOURCES

MAGAZINES AND NEWSPAPERS

*Air France Madame, Arts, Candide, Dépêche Mode, Dutch, Elle,
L'Express, Le Figaro, Focus, Gala, Glamour, Globe, L'Insensé,
Interview, The Japan Times, Jardin des Modes, Life Magazine,
Madame Figaro, Marie Claire, Men's Wear, Le Monde,
New York Magazine, Le Nouvel Observateur, The Observer,
Paris-Match, Le Point, Point de Vue, Saga, Tatler,
Témoignage Chrétien, Vogue Magazine US,
Vogue Magazine Paris, Women's Wear Daily, 20 ans.*

BOOKS

Histoire de la Photographie de mode (Nancy Hall-Duncan; Éditions
du Chêne, 1978) • *Yves Saint Laurent et le Théâtre* (Éditions Herscher –
Musées des arts décoratifs, 1982) • *YSL par YSL* (Éditions Herscher – Musée
des arts de la mode, 1986) • *Histoire technique et morale du vêtement*
(Maguelonne Toussaint-Samat; Bordas, 1990) • *Yves Saint Laurent*
(Laurence Benaïm; Grasset, 2002 and 2018) • *Yves Saint Laurent, 5 avenue
Marceau 75116 Paris* (David Teboul; Éditions de La Martinière, 2002)
• Exhibition catalogue, *Yves Saint Laurent, Dialogue avec l'art* (Fondation
Pierre Bergé – Yves Saint Laurent, 2004) • *Yves Saint Laurent Style*
(Éditions de La Martinière, 2008) • Exhibition catalogue, *Yves Saint
Laurent* au Petit Palais (Florence Müller, Farid Chenoune; Fondation Pierre
Bergé – Yves Saint Laurent, Éditions de La Martinière, 2010) • Exhibition
catalogue, *L'Asie rêvée d'Yves Saint Laurent* (Musée Yves Saint Laurent Paris,
éditions Gallimard, 2018).

TELEVISION

DIM DAM DOM via ORTF,
Fuji TV, Archives INA.

DOCUMENTARY FILM

Yves Saint Laurent: His Life and Times (2002),
written and directed by David Teboul.

★

Farewell speech by Yves Saint Laurent,
7 January 2002.

Archives du Musée Yves Saint Laurent Paris.

★

ABOUT THE AUTHORS

A writer, editor and journalist, Patrick Mauriès has published
numerous books and essays on art, literature, fashion
and the decorative arts. He has written about the unsung
creatives Piero Fornasetti, René Gruau and Line Vautrin,
and dedicated several books to figures ranging from
Jean-Paul Goude to Christian Lacroix and Karl Lagerfeld.

Jean-Christophe Napias is an author and editor, and in
2009 he founded the publishing house l'éditeur *singulier*
(The Singular Publisher). He has written many books about
Paris, most recently *Where to Find Peace and Quiet in Paris.*

Patrick Mauriès and Jean-Christophe Napias have
previously co-authored the Thames & Hudson books
*The World According to Karl, The World According to Coco,
The World According to Dior* and *Choupette: The Private Life
of a High-Flying Fashion Cat.*